Modern Curriculum Press
BEGINNING
TO
READ
Series

PLAY BALL

Margaret Hillert

Illustrated by Dick Martin

MODERN CURRICULUM PRESS

Pearson Learning Group

ISBN: 0-8136-5534-X
Printed in the United States of America

21 22 23 24 25 26   06 05 04 03 02

Modern
Curriculum
Press

Pearson Learning Group

1-800-321-3106
www.pearsonlearning.com

Do you want to play ball with me?
We can have fun.
I will run to my house and get a ball.

Now where is that ball?
Where did it go?
I have to find it.

Oh, here it is.
And here is something to go with it.
Now we can play ball.

Oh, no!

Look at you.

I guess we do not want this ball.

But I can get one that we will like.
I will run, run, run.
Do not go away.

No, no.
Get down.
Dogs can not play ball.
We want to play.

Here is the ball I want.
This one will work.
Here I come.

Oh, no!

What do I see now?

What do you have now?

We do not want this ball.
It is not the one for us.
What will we do?

Look, look.
I see something.
Is it a ball?

No, it is not a ball.
We can not play ball with it.
But it can go up.
See it go up.

19

Help, help!
Look at it go.
Away, away, away.

Oh, oh.

Down we come.

We do not like this.

Come to my house.

I have something that we can play with.

You will see.

Look at that.

I have a ball for that.

I will get it.

See this big ball.

It is fun to play with.

One, two, three.

26

And ———

UP!

Now you do it.

Do not look down.

Look up, and the ball will go up.

It can go up.
Up, up, and in.
Oh, my.
This is fun.

Jump, jump.
Get it in.
This is the ball for us.

Now we can play ball.
Now we can have fun.

Play Ball

Uses of This Book: Reading for fun. In this easy-to-read story two children want to play ball, but have some trouble deciding what kind of ball game to play.

Word List

All of the 58 words used in *Play Ball* are listed. Numbers refer to the page on which each word first appears.

5	do		my		something		come
	you		house	**9**	no	**15**	what
	want		and		look		see
	to		get		at	**16**	for
	play		a		guess		us
	ball	**6**	now		not	**17**	red
	with		where		this	**18**	up
	me		is	**11**	but	**21**	help
	we		that		one	**25**	big
	can		did		like		two
	have		it		away		three
	fun		go	**12**	down	**29**	in
	I		find		dogs	**30**	jump
	will	**8**	oh	**13**	the		
	run		here		work